Apes and Monkeys

KINGFISHER

a Houghton Mifflin Company imprint
222 Berkeley Street
Boston, Massachusetts 02116
www.houghtonmifflinbooks.com

First published in hardcover as *Kingfisher Young Knowledge: Apes and Monkeys* in 2004
First published in this format in 2007
2 4 6 8 10 9 7 5 3 1
1TR/0707/PROSP/RNB(RNB)/140MA/F

LIBRARY OF CONGRESS CATALOGING-IN-PUBLICATION DATA
Taylor, Barbara, 1954–
Apes and monkeys / Barbara Taylor.—1st ed.
p. cm.
1. Apes—Juvenile literature. 2. Monkeys—Juvenile literature. [1. Apes. 2. Monkeys.] I.
Title. II. Series.

QL737.P96T37 2004
599.88—dc22
2003069158

ISBN 978-0-7534-6163-1

Senior editor: Belinda Weber
Coordinating editor: Stephanie Pliakas
Designer: Carol Ann Davis
Cover designer: Jo Connor
Picture manager: Cee Weston-Baker
Picture researcher: Harriet Merry
DTP manager: Nicky Studdart
DTP operators: Primrose Burton, Claire Cessford
Artwork archivists: Wendy Allison, Jenny Lord
Senior production controllers: Nancy Roberts, Teresa Wood
Indexer: Chris Bernstein

Printed in China

Acknowledgments
The publishers would like to thank the following for permission to reproduce their material. Every care has been taken
to trace copyright holders. However, if there have been unintentional omissions or failure to trace copyright holders,
we apologize and will, if informed, endeavor to make corrections in any future edition.
b = bottom, *c* = center, *l* = left, *t* = top, *r* = right

Photographs: *cover* Getty; 4–5 Steve Bloom; 6–7 Oxford Scientific Films; 8 Martin Harvey/NHPA; 9 Ardea; 10–11 Ardea; 11*tl* Oxford
Scientific Films; 12*br* Oxford Scientific Films; 13*tl* Oxford Scientific Films; 14 Ardea; 15*t* Rojer Eritja/Alamy; 15*b* Steve Bloom; 16 Oxford
Scientific Films; 17 Steve Bloom; 18*b* Anup Shah/Nature Picture Library; 20*tr* Oxford Scientific Film; 22*b* Steve Bloom; 23*tr* Peter
Blackwell/Nature Picture Library; 23*l* Art Wolfe/Getty Images; 23*br* James Warwick/NHPA; 24*bl* Ardea; 24–25 Steve Bloom; 25*br* Ardea;
26*bl* Kevin Schafer/Corbis; 26*t* Tony Hamblin/Corbis; 29 Mark Bowler/NHPA; 30–31*b* Richard du Toit/NHPA; 31*tl* Anup Shah/Nature Picture
Library; 31 Roland Seitre/Still Pictures; 32*bl* Oxford Scientific Films; 32*br* Ardea; 33*tl* Oxford Scientific Films; 33*r* Anup Shah/Nature Picture
Library; 34*bl* Theo Allofs/Corbis; 34*r* Ardea; 35 Steve Bloom; 36*b* Anup Shah/Nature Picture Library; 36*t* Getty Images; 37*tl* Dietmar
Nill/Nature Picture Library; 37*b* Frank Lane Picture Agency; 38*b* Anup Shah/Nature Picture Library; 38*t* Ardea; 39 Getty Images;
40*tl* Ardea; 40*b* Karl Ammann/Nature Picture Library; 41 Ardea; 48 Steve Bloom

Commissioned photography on pages 42–47 by Andy Crawford. Project maker and photo shoot coordinator: Miranda Kennedy.
Thank you to models Aaron Hibbert, Lewis Manu, Alastair Roper, and Rebecca Roper.

Apes and Monkeys

Barbara Taylor

KINGFISHER
BOSTON

Contents

What is an ape?

You are one! There are four other great apes—gorillas, chimpanzees (chimps), orangutans, and bonobos. Gibbons are small apes. Apes have fingers and thumbs that can grip and no tail.

Hairy apes

Apes are a type of mammal, which is an animal with a hairy body. Hair helps keep mammals warm. We have much less hair than other apes such as this gorilla.

mammal—*a hairy animal that feeds its babies on its mother's milk*

Clever apes

All apes have big brains and are smart. They can solve problems, use tools, remember things, and communicate with each other. Humans are the only apes that can speak.

Arms and legs

Most apes' arms are longer than their legs. They can swing through the trees or walk on all fours. Humans walk upright on their long legs.

ommunicate—to make other animals understand your message

Apes in Africa

Three types of big wild apes live in the forests, woodlands, and mountains of Africa. These are gorillas, bonobos, and chimps. They all live in large groups.

Gorilla groups

Gorillas live in peaceful groups of between five and 20 member Each group of males, females, and young is led by a large male.

bonobo

chimpanzee

Girl power

Bonobos look like chimps but are more graceful. They have smaller heads and ears and longer legs than chimps. Female bonobos lead the groups.

Noisy chimpanzees

Chimps live in the biggest groups, with up to 100 members each. A few important male chimps lead each group. Chimps are noisier and fight more often than the other African apes.

forests—*places with many trees*

Apes in Asia

Orangutans and gibbons are apes that live in Asia. They spend a lot of time in trees, although male orangutans have to climb down sometimes when they grow too big for the branches.

Fat faces

Male orangutans have fatty pads that are the size of dinner plates on their faces. These pads make them look bigger and help them scare away any rivals.

rivals—*competitors for food or mates*

nging apes

Siamangs are the biggest
gibbons of all. They sing
in order to tell other gibbons
where they live. Pouches on
their throats inflate as they sing,
making their voices even louder.

inflate—to fill up with air

Moving around

Chimpanzees and gorillas spend a lot of time on the ground. Orangutans, gibbons, and bonobos climb in the trees. Gibbons live high up in the treetops.

Knuckle walking

When they walk on all fours, chimps rest their weight on thick pads of skin on their knuckles.

Swinging ape

Gibbons swing from branch to branch, first using one hand and then the other. They can move very quickly without making much noise.

Hanging on

Orangutans grip branches tightly with their long, hooked fingers. Their arms can stretch a long way. Each arm is almost twice as long as one of its legs!

knuckles—*places where the fingers bend*

Finding food

Apes feed mostly on fruit and leaves, but they also eat a small amount of meat such as insects. Chimps sometimes eat larger animals, including monkeys.

Going fishing!

Chimps chew on sticks or grass stems so they ca[n] make them the right sha[pe] to dig for food. They pus[h] the sticks into termite mounds. When they pull them out, termites are clinging to the ends.

Fruit feast

Durian is one of the orangutan's favorite foods. It can remember where to find trees with ripe fruit.

Tasty termites

Millions of termites live inside one termite mound. They can provide a tasty snack for hungry chimpanzees.

Clever apes

Apes are one of the few animals that can make and use tools, which is one sign of an intelligent animal.

Tough nuts to crack

Some chimps bang heavy stones on top of nuts. These stones work like hammers and crack open the nuts' hard shells.

Rainy days

Apes do not like the rain because their fur is not very waterproof. This orangutan has made its own umbrella using bark.

tools—*objects that help with work*

Chatty chimps

The chimpanzees in a group make different sounds, make faces, and use the positions of their bodies to "talk" to their family and friends.

Making faces

With their big eyes and flexible lips, chimps are good at making faces. Their expressions show how they are feeling.

Playtime

As young chimps play they learn how to get along with other chimps in their group. They also learn which chimps are the most important in the group.

Sound signals

Chimps use their big ears
to listen for sounds drifting
through the forest. The
members of a group
hoot to each other
to keep in touch.

Forever friends

Chimps may have special
friends in their group.
These friends hug each
other for comfort and
to show that they
are still friends.

expression—the "look" on a face

Baby apes

Apes usually have one baby at a time. They spend many years teaching the baby how to move, feed, and behave.

Gibbon families

Gibbons live in small family groups. A gibbon father plays with his baby and helps take care of it.

Riding piggyback

Many baby apes, such as this gorilla, are carried around until they are strong enough to walk by themselves.

Motherly love
A baby orangutan
lives with its mother
for seven to nine
years. It does not
usually have any
other playmates.

What is a monkey?

A monkey is a clever, playful mammal with a tail. It usually lives in groups for safety. There are 130 different monkeys, from tiny tamarins to big baboons.

Living space

Monkeys live in a wide range of habitats, from forests and mountains to grasslands and swamps. These proboscis monkeys live in a swamp.

errific tails

A monkey's tail can be long or short, thick or thin, straight or curly. This colobus monkey uses its fluffy tail to steer as it leaps through the trees.

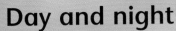

Day and night

The owl monkey is the only monkey that comes out at night. It has big eyes to help it see in the dark.

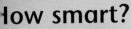

How smart?

Capuchins are intelligent monkeys with large brains. This helps them live in a range of different habitats.

habitats—areas where animals live

American monkeys

American monkeys live in the warm rain forests of Central and South America. They have wide, round nostrils that are far apart. Many have prehensile tails that can grip—almost like an extra hand.

Finger food

Tamarins have long fingers, which they use to search for their insect food. They have claws instead of fingernails.

Treetop leapers

Little squirrel monkeys leap through the trees like squirrels and climb onto thin branches. They live in big groups of up to 200 monkeys each.

Furry monkeys

Saki monkeys have long, shaggy fur, which helps protect them from heavy rain. They sometimes suck water off their fur.

rehensile tails—tails that can grip tightly

African and Asian monkeys

These monkeys have nostrils that are close together, along with hard pads on their bottoms to help them sleep sitting up. They do not have prehensile tails.

Packed lunch

The red-tailed monkey stores its food in its cheek pouches and then finds a safe place to sit down and eat.

Follow the leader

Slim, graceful mona monkeys live in troops of up to 20 monkeys each. Each troop is led by a strong male. Monas have bold marks and colors on their soft, thick fur.

Hot baths

Japanese macaques live in the mountains. In the cold, snowy winters they grow thick coats and sit in hot spring water to stay warm.

oop—a group of monkeys

Spot the difference

Monkeys are smaller than apes and are not as clever. Monkeys usually have tails, but apes never have tails.

Big ape

Gorillas are the biggest wild apes. Female gorillas weigh around half as much as male The size of the males scares away predators and rivals.

predators—animals that hunt and eat other animals

Monkey tails

A spider monkey curls its prehensile tail around a branch. The bare, ridged skin under the tail helps it cling on tightly.

Monkeys scamper along the tops of branches or run fast across the ground. They do not usually swing through the branches like apes.

Feet made for walking

Baboons live on the ground and walk on all fours. They press the fingers on the ground but keep their palms raised. This allows them to lift their heads so they can watch out for danger. They can even walk through water.

eggy leapers

The long back legs of colobus monkeys help them push off strongly from branches. They can make huge leaps from tree to tree.

Hanging around

Uakaris live at the tops of tall trees in swampy and flooded forests. They sometimes use their powerful back legs to hang upside down.

Hungry monkeys

A monkey's favorite food is usually fruit. Monkeys also eat leaves, nuts, flowers, and insects. Some have special diets, including marmosets, which eat tree gum (sap).

Nuts and seeds

Sakis spend a lot of time eating seeds. Some sakis have strong jaws to crack open hard nuts and reach the soft food stored inside.

Clever capuchin

This capuchin is chewing on bark from a small branch. It can also crack open nuts or shells by hitting them on top of rocks.

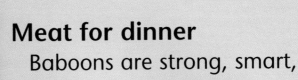

Meat for dinner

Baboons are strong, smart, and agile enough to be able to catch other monkeys, birds, and small antelope.

reen salad

Colobus monkeys mostly eat leaves, but they also enjoy munching on ripe fruit, flowers, and seeds. In their big stomachs bacteria release energy from their food.

bacteria—tiny, one-celled life-forms

33

Getting to know you

Monkeys have many ways of staying in touch. They use calls, colors, and behavior to find a mate and to warn of danger.

Stay away!

Howler monkeys are the world's noisiest land animals! Their calls warn other howlers to stay away.

Bad hair day?

Monkeys and apes groom each other fur. They pick out any dirt or bugs they find and clea up any scratches. Grooming helps monkeys stay clea and feel relaxed.

Color signals

The colors of the male mandrill become brighter when he is healthy, angry, or excited. Females prefer males with bright colors.

groom—to pick through fur with the fingers

Baby monkeys

Monkey mothers take care of their babies until they are around 12 to 18 months old—a shorter time than apes.

New babies
Baby monkeys have their eyes open at birth ar can cling onto their mother's fu

Baby-sitting
Langur mothers let oth females hold and take care of their babies. Thi makes their lives muc easier

Mother's milk

Like other mammals, vervet monkey mothers make milk in their bodies to feed to their babies. They have to eat a lot of food in order to give them enough energy to make this milk.

Watch and learn

Monkey babies, like this spider monkey, cling onto their mothers. They watch the other monkeys in the troop in order to learn how to climb and leap, which food is good to eat, and how to behave.

Apes and monkeys in danger

All apes (except humans) and many monkeys are in danger of becoming extinct. The main problem they face is humans.

Ape crisis

Almost all apes, including the white-handed gibbon, will be extinct in just 20 years. People must do more to save them from hunters and habitat destruction.

Disappearing act

Marmosets, like this tufted-ear marmose have lost their fores homes. They are also caught an sold as pets

Monkey madness

The rare Chinese golden monkey is threatened by hunting for its meat and fur. The trees in its forest home are also being cut down.

extinct—*none left alive anywhere on Earth*

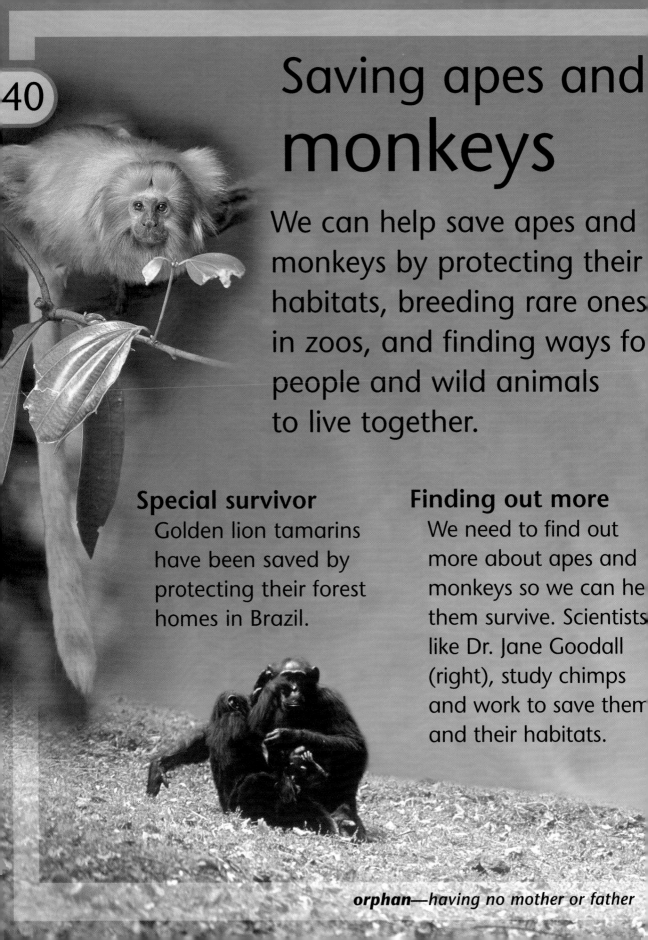

Saving apes and monkeys

We can help save apes and monkeys by protecting their habitats, breeding rare ones in zoos, and finding ways fo people and wild animals to live together.

Special survivor

Golden lion tamarins have been saved by protecting their forest homes in Brazil.

Finding out more

We need to find out more about apes and monkeys so we can he them survive. Scientists like Dr. Jane Goodall (right), study chimps and work to save them and their habitats.

orphan—having no mother or father

rphan apes

If a mother ape
dies or is killed,
her baby needs
a lot of love
and care. People
sometimes take
care of these
orphans and may
one day release them
back into the wild.

Monkey mobile

Make a monkey chain

Follow steps 1 through 5 to make one monkey. Then make more monkeys and hook their arms together in a long chain.

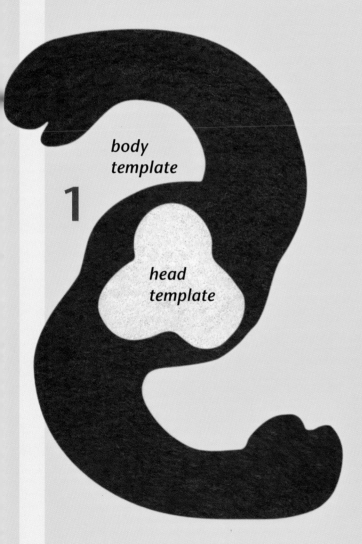

body template

1

head template

2

Using the scissors, carefully cut out the paper-plate templates. Hold the edge of the plate with one hand to stop it from moving.

3

Trace the two templates in pencil and transfer the outline shapes onto a paper plate.

Fold a piece of brown felt in half and secure it with a pin. Trace around the body template using a black marker and then cut it out.

You will need

- Tracing paper
- Pencil and black marker
- Paper plate
- Scissors
- Brown and cream felt
- Safety pin
- Glue

4

Glue the felt body shapes to the back and front of the paper-plate shapes. Make the faces using cream felt and glue them on.

5

Cut out four small "D" shapes and glue them on as ears. Use a black marker to draw on the eyes, nose, and mouth.

Termite towers

Eat like a chimpanzee

Make your own termite tower. Then put food inside and use a straw to get the food out. It is not as easy as it looks!

You will need

- Cardboard tubes
- Tape
- Scissors
- Paper plate
- Pencil
- Newspaper
- Glue or flour
- Water
- Paper towels
- Poster paints
- Paintbrush
- Candies
- Drinking straws

1 Find four clean cardboard tubes and tape them together. Ask a parent or friend to hold the tubes still while you do this.

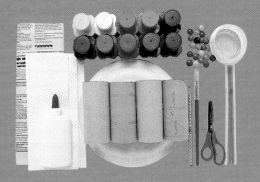

2 Turn a paper plate upside down. Hold the four tubes over the plate and trace around them using a pencil.

3 Using the scissors, carefully cut out the holes in the paper plate. Then tape the tubes firmly in place over the holes.

4

Crumple up pieces of newspaper and stick them into the gaps between the tubes. This should make a mound shape.

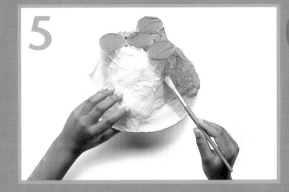

5

Mix flour and water together (or use glue) to stick strips of paper towels and newspaper over the mound. Paint the mound to look like mud.

Choose pieces of candy that are larger than the end of a straw and place them in the tubes. Suck through a straw to pull up the candies. How many can you catch?

Monkey masks

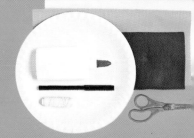

Make a monkey face

Monkeys and apes have round heads
that are perfect shapes for making masks.
Find your favorite monkey or ape in the
book and make a mask of its face.

You will need
- Pen
- Tracing paper
- Brown and white felt
- Scissors
- Glue
- Paper plate
- Rubber band

1

Draw the head of the monkey onto a
piece of tracing paper. Place this templ[ate]
onto some brown felt and carefully cut
around the outside edges.

2

Trace the face shape of the monkey
onto another piece of tracing paper.
Put this template over some light
brown felt and cut it out.

3

Glue the light brown felt on top
of the darker felt and stick them
both onto a paper plate. Glue
white felt rings around the eyes.

4

Glue on a felt nose and mouth.
Then cut out eyeholes and tie or
glue a rubber band to the sides
of the mask to hold it on.

Index